To Adrienne wishing you a lifetime of good books and wonderful Beach Adventures. Keep reading!

John Hutchinson 2017
Chatham

Bertie's Adventure

At the Beach

Written by John Hutchinson

Illustrated by Scout Hutchinson

&

John Hutchinson

🐦 *Hummingbird Publishing* 🐦

2016

ISBN 978-0-9833825-3-9 Hard Cover

Published by *Hummingbird Publishing*

Printed in the United States of America

To my mother

Harriet Jaqueth Fitz Hutchinson

The house he lived in was a cozy bungalow.

1

In a home on a farm near the sea lived a small field mouse named Bertie. The house he lived in was a cozy bungalow located between two fence posts at the edge of Farmer Brown's cornfield. Surrounded by grass and clover, much loved by bees and butterflies, it was well-hidden from intruders. In the front yard his mother kept a small garden in which she grew berries and vegetables.

The house was small and quite crowded when you consider that his father and mother and all his younger brothers and sisters lived there too. But in spite of these circumstances the family was comfortable and happy together.

Bertie's mother was a particularly fine cook.

Bertie's parents were loving and kind. His mother kept a tidy house, cool and airy in summertime and warm and cozy during the winter months. She was a particularly fine cook and her children never went hungry and never went to bed before they'd had a glass of fresh warm milk and a wedge of poppy seed pie or a gingerbread cookie.

From the farmyard his father was able to provide plenty of food for the family dining table. He was an excellent judge of grain and seeds and never failed to bring home a bit of cake or other sweet from Mrs. Brown's pantry.

They had only a few rules for their children: avoid mouse traps, keep clear of cats and never go to the seashore without their mother or father. Some years ago Bertie's uncle had taken three of his children to the beach. They did not return that evening. In the days that followed there had been much talk around the farmyard of foxes or wild cats or hawks, and even whispers that they might have been swept out to sea when they had gone swimming. The sad fact remained that they had never come home.

But that was long ago. Bertie knew there were many wonderful things to be seen at the beach as well as dangers that a small and inexperienced mouse should avoid. He had heard tales from older friends about the strange and wonderful creatures who lived there. He yearned to see them for himself. Although he and his brothers and sisters were very good at obeying rules they overflowed with curiosity. Alas, their parents seemed always to be too busy to have time to take them to that fabled place. Bertie suspected that they remembered the fate of his uncle and cousins and wished to have no part of such a dangerous spot.

Now, this was a bit strange to Bertie because he knew well that his father was descended from a long line of seafaring mice and had served in the officers' wardroom aboard a great navy battleship. On that ship he had lived behind the galley wall next to the stove. It had been his duty to keep the wardroom cooking area spotless and crumb-free. He had retired from the sea after many years of honorable service and had married, settled down ashore, and started a family in his home at the edge of the cornfield. But he treasured fond memories of his life at sea. In the evenings Bertie and his brothers and sisters would gather about his overstuffed chair while he warmed his rheumatic feet in front of the cottage fireplace and spun wonderful yarns about his ocean voyages and the battles his ship had fought. His parents had given him a fine library of sea stories which he kept in stacks in his bedroom.

A fine library of sea stories.

These he had read and reread until their covers were worn and their pages tattered and dog-eared. As he read them thoughts of dangerous exploits and narrow escapes filled his imagination. If his father had enjoyed so many adventure-filled years as a young mouse, then certainly he was ready to begin such a life. This ho-hum existence around the farmyard was becoming tame, sometimes even boring, for him. Surely he was old enough to take care of himself even if his parents didn't think he could. Why, just last week hadn't he outsmarted the wily old barn cat who thought he'd had Bertie cornered in the stable hayloft? There wasn't one of Farmer Brown's mousetraps he hadn't sprung to steal the cheese. No harm had come from these exploits. Now that he was grown up Bertie had begun to think of himself as an adventuresome and even daring young mouse. There was so much of the world beyond the farmyard that he wished to see. An expedition to the seashore would be a good first step toward his becoming a more worldly mouse. He was determined to go.

2

And so it was that one warm and lovely morning as the sun was climbing up in the blue sky, and his father had gone to the nearby barn to get the family dinner, and his mother was hanging the laundry on her clothesline, Bertie decided that today was the day he was going to visit the seashore.

He slipped away under the hedge, sped through the cornfield, darted beneath the branches of the trees in the apple orchard, dashed across the green meadow, then scurried down a narrow path, through some very tall grass and, suddenly, there

It stretched away as far as he could see.

before him lay a broad sweep of white sand. Spread
beyond that was an endless expanse of blue water.

It stretched away, all sparkly and danc-
ing, for as far as he could see before it touched the
sky. As his eyes took in the broad vista before
him, he felt the breath all but rush from his small
breast. Now, this glorious sight was worth dis-
obeying his parents to see! He stood rooted among

the sparse beach grass marveling at this extraordinary scene but afraid to venture beyond onto the sand.

'So,' he thought, 'this is the great ocean upon which my father sailed and fought in famous battles! At last I'm seeing it. Oh, how glorious if one day I could sail on it in a ship of my own!'

He had been admiring this marvelous view for quite a while, imagining himself voyaging to distant places and wishing he could summon up the courage to step out onto the beach, when a very large white bird floated gracefully down from the sky and settled onto the sand close by. As it began to walk toward him Bertie turned to dash back into the tall grass. Just then the bird called out to him in a rough but kindly voice, "Ahoy there, little matey! Me name's Sebastian Seagull. What be yers and what be yer doin' here?"

The large bird seemed so friendly that Bertie hesitated, then turned around and said, "I'm Bertie and I live beyond the orchard next to the cornfield with my father and mother and brothers and sisters."

I'm Bertie.

"Aye! I know yer parents. They be Mr.
and Mrs. Matthew Fieldmouse. An' what can a
wee mouse such as yerself be doin' here s' far from
home?"

"I've come to explore the seashore. My
parents say it's dangerous but it doesn't look scary
to me. I would so love to go out there to the water

but I admit I am a bit afraid to go without anything around to hide under. It's such a long way."

"Well," said the old gull. "I knows me way 'round these parts like the back o' me wing. I c'n show yer about that beach ef y'd like ter take a stroll. I'd make sure no harm'd come to yer. Y' must stick close t' me as a limpet fer this beach can be a dangerous place fer sech a small critter as yerself. Jest step alongside o' me and we shall see some interestin' sights."

So Bertie scuttled under Sebastian's wing and off they went to visit the new world that lay before him.

It cried out Weeee!

3

As Bertie trotted along beside his guide he kept a sharp lookout for any sign of this "danger" and at the same time his eyes were drinking in the many new sights and sounds and smells. All at once from out of the sand directly in front of them sprang up a tiny pale creature.

It cried out "Weeeeee!"

Astonished, Bertie stopped short. This strange creature was jumping from the sand high up over their heads and then landing nearby and popping back into the air like a tiny rubber ball. With every leap it cried out "Weeeeeeee!" and landed, and then POP! up over Bertie's head it soared again.

As it made each bound it gave another "Weeeeeeee!"

Bertie watched in amazement for he had never seen anything like this small acrobat. When he had recovered from his surprise he called out, "Hey there you bouncing spitball! Could you please stop that jumping about for a moment and tell me who you are."

At that, the creature made several smaller jumps toward them and landed right beside Bertie. "Whew!" the small thing gasped. "That sure is fun but it does get tiring after a while."

It was as curious a looking creature as Bertie had ever seen. He was quite familiar with small insects like horseflies and bees and ants, but this fellow was altogether very different and strange looking. The size and color of one of the large delicious peanuts that his father sometimes brought home, it sported what appeared to be stripes across its back, a pair of long antennae and two rather large round eyes.

"Hey!" exclaimed Bertie, "Just hold on for a moment! Tell me your name and why you are doing all that jumping about."

"Because it's funnnnnnnn!" answered the small creature, and gave a little hop. "And my name is Sammy Sandflea. All of us sand fleas live under the sand to hide from danger. When it's safe to come up to play we pop out of our hiding places and leap about like kangaroos."

"But how is such a tiny fellow as yourself able to leap so high into the air?" asked a bewildered Bertie.

"Because I have very strong springs in my legs and toes. I can jump up to a hundred times my height if I want to. Like this… "Wheeeeee!" And he sprang up into the air and away.

"My goodness, Sebastian," said Bertie. "What strange creatures live on this beach."

"Right-o, shipmate. There be many more interestin' sights for yer eyes ter see," replied the old gull. "Come along, me little hearty, fer we've just begun our sightseein' tour," and he started down the beach toward the water with Bertie trotting behind, his little patty paws going as fast as they could to keep up.

4

The sand was becoming softer and Bertie's feet began to sink down into it with each step. This made for slower going. He kept lagging behind and having to scurry to catch up. Often Sebastian stopped, looked over his shoulder and called out "Come along with ye, Bertie. We needs ter get t' the water's edge afore the tide runs out any further," and Bertie would scamper up to him, huffing and puffing to catch his breath.

Soon they had left the soft deep sand behind. Bertie asked, "Why is the sand becoming damp, Sebastian? We're still a long way from the water."

"That's on account o' the sea water travels under the sand. It slips along silent-like from the ocean's edge toward the dry land a good ways further 'n y'd think. Though ya can't see water under the sand at yer feet, if y' were t' dig down a few inches right here y'd find salt water. An' there be lots of wee critturs livin' in it."

"Will we be meeting any of them, Sebastian?" he asked hopefully.

"Can't promise yer anythin'," replied his friend. "Let's jest keep forgin' ahead with our eyes peeled, an' we shall see what we shall see."

As Bertie glanced around he saw, strewn over the beach in every direction, all manner of dried up crinkly stuff, clumps of dead grass, pebbles, bottles, bits of rope, strange looking pieces of wood, shiny jagged objects that looked like bits of broken rock and many small pieces of white stuff. These last reminded him of the tasty cracker morsels which from time to time his father would bring home from the farmhouse kitchen. Expecting a sweet treat he picked up one of these delicious looking tidbits and nibbled at its edge.

He picked up one of these delicious looking tidbits.

"IKKKKHH!" he cried and spit it out, for it was as hard as a stone and had no taste at all. "What's this awful stuff, Sebastian? It looks so delicious but it hurts my teeth and tastes like a stone!"

"Bertie, y're a funny little mouse," the gull laughed, "That thar's a piece o' broken seashell, all what's left o' one o' the many, many former residents what once lived hereabouts in the sand an' in the waters near by t' this here beach. Gone to their reward now, be they, but they've left behind their protective jackets. I tells yer, them seashells is no good fer eatin'."

Disgusted, Bertie was tossing the bit of clamshell over his shoulder when he saw a very strange and scary looking creature rushing sideways across the sand towards the water. He turned to Sebastian. "What the heck is that?" he asked.

"That be Mr. Crab," said Sebastian and he held up a wing. "Avast thar, Cranky! " he called out. The crab immediately came to a halt and crouched stiffly with its forearms in front of its face in a menacing gesture as if prepared for a fight. "Whar be yer off ter in sech a hurry? I wants ter introduce me friend, Bertie, t' yer."

"I've no time for any social rubbish, Sebastian. Can't you see I'm in a rush?"

" O'course I can, y' cranky old crustacean. But Bertie here'd be pleased ter make yer aquaitance. Come over here close aboard ter us an' we'll have us a gam. No harm'll come ter ye, I warrant."

Keep your distance, Bratty.

"Keep your distance. You too Bratty, or Bertie, or whatever your name is!" he burbled. As he spoke bubbles were frothing out from the place where Bertie thought his mouth should be. "You're not fooling me for a minute, Sebastian. I know what you're up to—you and your sneaky ways." The ornery crab blustered on and waved his claws wildly, which gave Bertie a considerable fright. "Let me warn you, I'm in no mood to have it out with you just now. With one pinch of my claw here I could...."

"Shiver me timbers, Cranky! No need fer all yer carryin' on so. Y've got yerself into a fine pickle, now," Sebastian chuckled. "Y're findin' yerself with too much beach 'tween yerself an' the water's edge. Y' be far from yer element, bucko, and y'd be no match fer me if I'd a hankerin' ter make a meal o' yer, I'm thinkin'. An' I'd make fast work o' ye, too, yer can bet yer six boots on it. But I'm presently out fer a peaceful stroll with me new shipmate here an' will have no cause t' bother with yer on this partica'ly fine day, y' c'n thank yer stars fer that."

"Whatever," the crab replied with false bravado. "You two keep your distance if you know what's good for you. I could turn your small friend into fish food in a few seconds, Sebastian, if you weren't around, you big bully. But I'll just be scuttling along now. I want to get my dinner before the tide goes out further," and with that he rushed off toward the water on his prancey toes.

"Oh, my," Bertie exclaimed. "What a fierce fellow Sebastian! I'm so glad you were here. Who was that strange creature?"

"That blowhard? That's Old Cranky. He's a member o' the Blue Crab family. They're mighty sav'ry eatin', I tells ya, but I've jest had me break-fast so I let him have safe passage."

"He's sure a weird looking creature with those funny eyes on sticks, and what an ugly mouth. And all those legs! They move so fast when he runs. They're a blur. And what were those big pincher things that go where his front paws should be?"

"Them's his claws. He uses 'em t' eat with an' t' fight off boardin' attackers if any comes along-side o' him."

"UGGHHH!" said Bertie with a fearful shudder. "I'd hate it if he grabbed my nose with those nasty claws."

"He's all smoke 'n' fire but thur's no can-non shot to 'im. He wouldn't hurt ye unless y' tried to harm 'im. Them crabs don't care fer live mouse meat, anyways. The prefers dead stuff they finds in thur travels," Sebastian added. "Let's be gettin' along now."

5

They had gone only a few steps when Bertie stopped and, appearing to have come to a realization, said, "Well, I'd better do my best to be careful here." He then looked up at his new friend and added, "But while we're on this rather distasteful subject, Sebastian, what do you eat here on the beach?"

"Oh, I eats pretty much anythin' I c'n get me bill around, Bertie. We seagulls is a tribe o' what yer calls "scavengers." We eats most anythin' we c'n find around the sea shore, dead 'r alive. It don't matter much t' us gulls what it is s' long 's we c'n digest it. But clam shells is one item that's not on our menu."

"Oh my!" exclaimed Bertie. "This beach is a far more dangerous place than I imagined, Sebastian. It seems to me that everyone is eating someone else out here." He paused for a long moment before adding in a hesitant voice "I-I don't suppose you eat small field mice, do you?"

"I-I don't suppose you eat small field mice, do you?"

"Not I, young feller," he replied with a chuckle. "We gulls prefers sea critturs when we gets ter choose. Fish 'n' crabs 'n' clams be our favorites, though most anythin' 'll do in a pinch. If'n we're not at the beach, why, garbage dumps does jest fine fer a change o' pace, like. Plenty fer a self-respectin' seagull t' eat over t' the landfill. In fact, when it comes t' sumthin' else 'sides seafood, the dump's me favorite dinin' spot, fer there's not much work ter findin' a good square meal there. All kinds o' lip-smackin' goodies an' no work t' gettin' 'em, 'ceptin' for fightin' off me friends when I finds a particar'ly juicy bit o' swill."

"Oh, don't say so, Sebastian! How disgusting! My friends the rats have told me about the stuff that's in that dump. How could you ever think of eating there?"

"Well, young feller, 'Each ter his own,' says the farmer an' he kissed his pig. Thur's food fit fer a king an' plenty of it, thereabouts. An' by the by, y've got no reason t' fear old Sebastian fer he's on a strict vegetarian kick these days—on me confounded doct'r's orders. I bin experiencin' a severe case o' the collywobbles lately, so he's taken red meat of any kind off me diet."

"That's a relief! I've been a bit worried for a while," said Bertie, and on they went.

"Hey, geysers!"

6

As they got closer to the ocean Bertie was surprised to see tiny spurts of water squirt up out of the sand all around him in small showers that wet his fur and gave him a bit of a fright.

"Hey, geysers!" he cried out. "What's making all those fountains?"

"Why, them's the Clam Clan—Clarence, Clarissa, Clyde and Clayton and all thur other children," answered Sebastian. "They felt us comin' an' that's thur way of sayin' 'Hello' t' us by sayin' 'Goodbye.'"

"But why are they under the sand and where'd they go?" asked Bertie.

"They lives down there t' keep safe from thur enemies, me lad," explained Sebastian. "If someone comes t' harm 'em they gives a big squirt, in a manner o' speakin', and shoots deep down inter thur tunnels quick-like, t' where few enemies c'n get at 'em. Them fellers spends thur whole lives underneath the sand in thur damp homes where they be safe from predators."

"Just like a mouse in a deep mouse hole, I would say," replied Bertie and on they went.

"Right-o, Bertie. Jest so."

"What do they look like and what do they eat?" Bertie inquired.

"Well, thur insides is all soft 'n' squishy, but the best eatin' around this beach. I warrant yer. On thur outside they wears a hard white shell. It looks a bit like a some'at squished ball what's bin stretched out at one end. Ya hardly ever sees 'em on account o' they spends thur whole lives down in thur holes. If, by chance, ya catches one lyin' on the sand outside his door he's more 'n likely passed on t' the Great Clam Flats above." he continued; "As fer feedin' thurselves they eats in a strange way. It's like this. With thur on-board pumps they sucks in seawater, which contains millions o' ever-so-small critturs, into thur stomachs. Then they strains them little goodies by a kind o' filter system an' then squirts out the used water."

"One of those squirt holes for each clam, Sebastian? If they never come out of their holes they must get very lonely."

"They leads lives o' splendid isolation. They be happiest when the tide's high an' they's restin' snug at the bottom o' thur tunnels, fer very few enemies can git at 'em when they be under a fathom o' sea water. Once in a while I catches one at low tide and grabs him afore he c'n dig his self down his hole out o' my reach. Mighty fine eatin' they be, I warrant."

"But how are you able to catch them if they're under the sand?" asked Bertie.

"Well, ya see, I sneaks up on 'em all tippy-toe an' quiet-like, on the lookout fer one o' them holes they makes. If I feels 'em move with me feet, or sees 'em squirtin' up the way we did jest now, I knows I'm in luck. Swift as lightnin' I plunges me bill into the sand. If'n I'm fast enough I catches 'em afore they c'n start down, an' hauls 'em outta thur hole. Gotta be quick, though. Them clams is some speedy."

"But if their shells are so hard, Sebastian, how do you get them open?"

"Ah! Good question, Bertie lad. Yer be a smart 'un," he replied. "If I can't pry thur shells apart with me bill I carries 'em aloft. Then I flies over to one o' me favorite clam-bustin' spots, such as a bunch o' large rocks or a bit o' paved road, an' then I lets 'em fall. Down they goes on thur last flight an' when they hits the hard surface thur shells burst wide open. Then I c'n feast on thur insides t' me heart's content, leavin' thur shells behind, o' course."

"Ugh!" Bertie exclaimed. "You eat them after they've broken apart all over the road?"

"Us gulls ain't too persnickity about our table manners. We eats our meals any place we finds 'em. Ya might call us scavengers. An' them clams be prize eatin', I c'n tell yer. All sweet an' tender-like. But enough o' this gabbin' away like a couple o' old fishwives. Thur's plenty jest ahead for us ter see."

7

It wasn't long before they found themselves at the water's edge. Bertie stood gazing out onto the ocean. Such an enormous body of water! Of course he had seen small rain puddles and deeper water in the horse trough by the corral, but this great shimmering expanse that stretched as far as his eyes could see—No. This was quite different.

After a while he looked up at Sebastian and asked in a voice filled with awe, "Might I touch it, Sebastian? It looks so beautiful."

"Might I touch it, Sebastian?"

"Certainly y' may," the gull replied and watched as his friend leaned down to tentatively thrust his paw into the clear liquid.

"Mmmmmmmmmm, it feels so inviting," Bertie exclaimed. "I wonder how it tastes?" he added. Before Sebastian could warn him he had squatted down, made a little cup with his paw and scooped up some water.

Bertie's paw-cup was at his whiskery mouth.

"Avast thar, Bertie...!" Sebastian began and held up a wing. But before he could say another word Bertie's paw-cup was at his whiskery mouth and he was drinking from it.

"YUUHHHHCK!" he cried and spit it all out. "AARRRGGGHHHH! That tastes terrible! How could such lovely looking stuff have such a bitter taste?"

Sebastian gave a chuckle. "I tried to warn yer, Bertie. The sea is made o' salt water an' tastes mighty sour. Meself, I'm used t' salt water an' washes down me meals with it, but if I was yerself I'd keep it out o' me mouth. On the other hand, if y'd like yer might take a little swim in it."

"But my fur would get all wet."

"Aye, it would, though under this warm sun yer fur would dry in two shakes of a shark's tail."

Just then, before Bertie could decide whether a swim might be a good idea, a flock of small birds flashed past them just overhead. They made odd peeping cries and chitter-chattered among themselves as they dipped and wheeled in a tight formation. Then in a twinkling, as if they were a single body, they landed almost at the same moment, it seemed, and commenced to skitter and jitter about here and there while jabbing their long bills into the wet sand.

"Come on," said Sebastian. "Ferget about any swimmin' fer the moment. We'll see what news our feathered friends might have fer us."

8

As they drew near to the group of chittering brown and white birds, one detached itself from the group and headed their way.

"Good morning, Sebastian, old friend. Nice to seep-seep-see you here on our stretch of the beep-beep-beach. What are you up to?"

"Oh, I'm showin' me new friend, Bertie here, the wonders o' the beach," the gull replied. "Bertie, meet Sandy Sandpiper. She an' I reg'larly dines together 'round these parts when the tide be out."

"Hi. My name's Bertie."

Boldly, Bertie greeted the stranger. "Hi. My name's Bertie."

"It's a peep-peep-peep pleasure to meep-meep-meet you, Bertie. My friends and I have dropped in here for a leep-leep-leisurely lunch."

"Do you often come here to eat?"

"Oh yes," Sandy replied. "We have found this peep-peep-peaceful spot particularly inviting. Lots to dine on along theep-theep-these flats."

"It looks to me as though what you're eating is a lot of wet sand," observed Bertie. "That can't be very tasty."

"Oh, heep-heep-hee!" laughed the shorebird. "That's very funny, Bertie. It just looks that way. Actually wee-wee-we are delving for our lunch under the surface of the flats with our bills. Beep-beep-beneath this wet sand are many very small and tasty creatures. We locate them with our bills and pull them up. Mmmm-mmm. Excellent dining hereabouts." She started off to rejoin her friends.

"Hold on there a bit, would ye, Sandy. I suspect ya bin up an' down along the shore t'day. Have y' seen anythin' in yer travels what might be of interest t' me wee friend here?" Sebastian asked.

"Hmm," replied the sandpiper. "Well, not far up the coast there are the bones of an old shipwreck that the last storm uncovered. But that would beep-beep-be a long walk for your little friend."

She thought for another moment and added, "A few peep-peep-people are digging for clams beep-beep-beyond those sand dunes, and a group of men are fishing in the surf way down the beep-beep-beach. A while ago wee-wee-we flew over Mister Fox over there beep-beep-behind you. He was peep-peep-peeking over a sand dune in hopes of catching the Plover family off their guard. Oh, and come to think of it, wee-wee-we saw Henry Hawk soaring above the lighthouse. Better keep-keep-keep your eyes peep-peep-peeled and beep-beep-be on the lookout for him."

"We'll be sure ter keep a watchful eye out fer Foxy an' that old buzzard, Henry," Sebastian said. "Well, time t' be uppin' our anchor and on our way. We wish yer good eatin'. "

"Oh, thank you, Sebastian. It was a pleasure to meep-meep-meet you, Bertie."

"And I fee-fee-feel the same, Sandy," and when she had gone he looked up with a grin to see if Sebastian approved of his joke.

"Now, Bertie, don't be makin' fun o' other folks' failin's," Sebastian scolded with a trace of a smile on his face. They turned away to resume their stroll as the sandpiper skittered off to rejoin her friends.

9

As they made their way along the water's edge, Bertie's eyes continued to drink in the many new sights. All about them were birds he had never seen. They flew every which way above and around them and called out to each other and occasionally greeted Sebastian. And all those strange bits of stuff about them in the sand; strands of weeds and pieces of bone and weird stick-like things. Whatever could they all be?

He pestered Sebastian with questions

about all that he was seeing. The patient old gull answered his every question and never spoke a cross word to him.

As they went along, the sun continued its climb ever higher up the sky. Looking out across the water Bertie asked, "Sebastian, I don't understand. The water's so clear when I look straight down but when I look out into the distance it's blue."

"Oh, that's an easy one," the gull responded. "Y' see, the water's got no color to it. It's clear as a glass, but like a mirror 's well, ya might say, so's when yer looks out acrost it t' the horizon it looks blue. That's 'cause what yer seein's a reflection o' the sky in it."

"Wow. That's interesting." Bertie imagined, explaining this piece of new information to his brothers and sisters.

The day was growing warmer by the moment and Bertie soon began to feel uncomfortably hot. Unable to restrain himself any longer he looked up and asked, "It's so beautiful, Sebastian, and it looks so wonderfully cool and inviting. Might I wade out into it a short way?"

"O' course yer can. 'Twon't harm ya none, but stay close by the shore in the shaller water. The currents is tricky an' dangerous jest here an' yer can't tell what manner o' critturs might be lurkin' b'neath the surface," the gull replied.

He watched as the little mouse took a hesitant step into the shallow water. Bertie stopped and gave his foot a shake and then, being the daring little mouse that he was, he put it in again and then his other foot.

The little mouse took a hesitant step into the shallow water.

The cool water around his feet seemed to urge him to venture into deeper water. In a moment, he had forgotten about his fear of getting his fur wet and Sebastian's warning, for now his body almost ached to lie down and refresh itself in this cool water.

At last, unable to bear it any longer he said "Oh, Sebastian, I am so hot. Could I go out just a bit deeper? I yearn to dunk myself into this shallow water." He added, "Doesn't this heat bother you?"

"No, shipmate. Old Sebastian's used ter it. Me feathers provides me with excellent insulation against hot an' cold weather alike." He went on, "Go ahead an' jump right in but stay close ter the shore. There be hungry fishes out there in the deeper water. They'd be mighty pleased ter pull a tasty mouse like yerself under an' gobble him down in a single bite."

"Oh, I'm not at all afraid. I promise to be careful, Sebastian, and to stay in the shallow water." And with that he skipped out into its wonderful coolness.

"Oh boy! This is fantastic!" cried Bertie as he splashed about and waded in deeper. How refreshing this water felt as it closed over his tiny legs. How delightful it was to see the hundreds of drops of water glisten in the sun as they flew upward from his feet and legs. In no time the water was up to his waist and soon it closed over his chest. Tentatively he lay his body into the water. It felt so cool on his hot fur. The next thing he knew his feet were off the bottom and he was floating!

"Paddle with yer paws but don't go out too deep!" Sebastian called after him. "Yer'll get out over yer head an' discover yer can't swim an' that'll be the end of our fun jaunt on the beach!"

But Bertie's feet were already paddling along in the deliciously cool ocean water. After just a few wild splashes his little paws began to work in a productive and exhilarating way and before he knew it he was swimming.

10

"Oh boy, Sebastian, look at me. I'm swimming!" he called back to his friend. Rolling over onto his back he struck out into deeper water. "This water is so refreshing and this swimming is the best feeling. I could do it forever!"and he added, "I feel so free!"

"Wonderful, Bertie," Sebastian called. "But afore y' get too far out y' might change yer course an' head closer to the shore. Remember about them hungry fishes what lurks out there."

"Oh Sebastian, don't be such a spoil sport. I don't see any fishes around me," he called back brazenly. "And anyway, how could something so wonderful as swimming in this lovely water be dangerous? It's the absolute best. I feel as light as a feather!"

Bertie found himself cruising joyfully along as his paws propelled him ahead with little effort. Never had anything felt this marvelous. As he splashed and frolicked he paid little mind to the distance that was opening between him and the shore, or to those words of warning Sebastian had spoken back on the beach.

"Now, Bertie, git yerself back closer to the shore. Y' be too far out," Sebastian called out sternly now. Suddenly he was sounding an awful lot like Bertie's father. So, being an obedient sort of a young mouse he reluctantly began to paddle toward his friend.

But what he had imagined would be a short swim was quickly turning into a bit of a struggle. It appeared that, try as he might, he was not getting any closer to Sebastian and the shallow water. In fact, he could see that despite his efforts he was being carried farther and farther away from the shore. He worked his little legs faster and faster, yet his friend was getting smaller and smaller. Suddenly his joyous feeling of swimming had turned to fear, and in the next moment to terror.

"Help! Help! I'm going out to sea."

"Help! Help!" Bertie cried out. "I am going out to sea.

"Swim along the shore so yer can come in gradual-like, y' foolish mouse, not right at me!" Sebastian called back to him. "That's the best way t' reach the shaller water."

But the current was carrying Bertie farther away from the shore. In his panic he failed to understand what Sebastian meant. With all four paws he struck out frantically toward the gull but to no avail.

But now water was splashing up into his nose and eyes, and some got into his mouth causing him to gasp and choke. His arms and legs were growing weaker by the second. It was all he could do to turn himself over onto his back in order to float and rest for a moment. Sebastian was looking ever smaller and Bertie was feeling ever more desperate.

In a flash he pictured his uncle and three cousins being swept out to sea. 'If I drown,' he thought, 'no one will ever know what has become of me. Oh, why did I ever disobey my parents?'

11

Bertie was exhausted. As he floated and rested for a moment he thought 'I'll try to do what Sebastian told me,' and he began to follow the seagull's advice. Almost at once he discovered that he could swim more easily by not heading directly toward the beach against the strong current and waves.

'Whew!' he thought, 'Perhaps I'll make it to the shore after all. But I'm growing ever more weary.' His little legs were still churning slowly and painfully yet the shore seemed no nearer. 'At this rate I'll soon be so weak that I'll no longer be able to stay afloat. I'll sink to the bottom among the hungry crabs and fishes or be swept out to sea.'

At that moment the thought of his brave father, who had never surrendered when faced with danger, flashed into Bertie's mind. He said to himself with fresh resolve, 'I won't give up. It's better to go down swimming than to give in. I'll fight on until my arms and legs refuse to move. As long as I can stay above water I have a chance.' And after a few moments it seemed that he might have swum a bit closer to the shore. Yes, Sebastian did seem to have grown larger, but it was still such long way for his tired legs to propel him.

'Oh, dear,' he thought. 'If only I had listened to my mother and father I would not be in this frightful mess. I don't know how much longer I can go on. If I don't rest again then I'll go under and never again see my beloved home and family.'

These gloomy thoughts were crowding into his head when all at once he felt his hind foot touch something that felt like solid ground. In another moment his second foot touched. He thought, 'I must have come upon a large submerged rock, for I'm standing on something quite solid. Can it be that I'm saved?'

Although only his head was above water he was able to rest and take some deep breaths. It was still a long way to where Sebastian stood but at least now he could rest his aching legs.

'What good fortune!' he thought. 'I'll be able to gather my strength and when I am rested I shall be able to try to make it back to the shore.'

He called out to his friend, "I'm okay now, Sebastian. I've found a rock on which I can stand."

He felt the rock begin to move.

12

At that very moment he felt the rock be-gin to move.

'My goodness! I've never known a rock to move by itself,' he thought. Just a little bit but, yes, he could feel that it definitely was moving. And sure enough, although he was standing quite still he could feel himself moving through the water. This was very strange. Supposing his safe perch began to head out into deeper water? He would have to start this tiring swimming again and before long his head would go under water and he would be lost indeed!

But, no! His rock seemed to be making its way slowly but surely toward the beach.

'Whew!' he said to himself. 'By what strange magic am I being rescued?' For it appeared that this was exactly what was happening.

Now his shoulders were above the water. Before long he could see his waist. And look! There was Sebastian growing larger every moment. Bertie could hear him chuckling. "Well, Bertie, looks t' me like the sea decided it didn't want ter take yer away t'day after all. In fact, it looks like it's fetched yer back t' me."

By this time the water around him had become so shallow that Bertie could see his knees. As he peered down through the clear liquid he could see that his moving rock was actually a large dark form shaped like one of those horseshoes he often came across around the barn.

In another moment the top of his rock was clear of the water. With a cry of joy and relief Bertie leaped from his perch and dashed to Sebastian. He was so happy to be on dry land and safe that he threw both his tiny arms around the old gull's leg and hugged it tightly.

"Oh, Sebastian," he cried. "Never was I happier to see an old friend!"

"And m'self, 's well, Bertie. Fer a minute I figgered me new shipmate fer a goner," replied the gull. "Welcome back from yer ocean adventure, ya foolhardy field mouse. Look behind yer at yer rescuer an' thank him."

Bertie turned and was astonished to see that his "rock" had emerged from the water and sat very rock-like a short distance away. What a strange sight was this large object! In fact, it was alive and moving toward them.

"H-hello Mr. Horace."

13

"Bertie," said Sebastian, "Meet Mr. Horace Horseshoecrab."

Bertie approached this forbidding creature with some anxiety. He paused and then declared in an uncertain voice. "H-hello, Mr. Horace. I will be forever grateful to you for saving my life. I'd have been swept out to sea if you had not arrived underneath my feet at the right moment."

"The pleasure was all mine, Bertie," the crab replied in a deep rumbly voice that sounded as though it were coming from a cave at the bottom of the sea. "But our meeting was nothing more than a happy accident. I was simply strolling along the ocean floor headed ashore for dinner when you came aboard me. You are so small and light that I didn't realize you were standing on top of me until I saw you leap off into the shallow water. Glad to be of service, though."

Bertie found himself staring rather impolitely at this strange creature who rested so solidly on the sand. It couldn't be said that Horace "stood" there, for he apparently had no feet. He was huge, as large as Sebastian—so much bigger than Bertie. His color was dark, almost black, and he sported a row of pointed things along his back as well as a long and terrible-looking sharply pointed tail. This was indeed an unusual and terrible looking beast, but for one so awful looking, its voice, though deep and hollow sounding, was gentle.

Before he could remember his manners Bertie blurted out "But if you have no feet, Mr. Horace! How can you move about on the sea floor and in the water and on the sand?" and then he added, for he had been brought up by a polite mother and father, "If you'll forgive my asking, please."

"Oh, that's an easy one," replied Horace. "I have many feet beneath this shell of mine. Some are made for walking on dry land or the sea bottom, while others are designed for swimming. I am quite thoroughly adapted to my environment."

"Well," responded Bertie, "You must be a wonderful and dangerous fighter." Forgetting his manners momentarily he went on, "You look like a tank with no treads; and with that long sword attached at your rear you're quite frightful."

"That's what many folks think but my tail's not for fighting. It just looks dangerous. It's a bit like another leg," Horace replied with a deep chuckle. "If I get turned upside down by the action of the waves or by an enemy, I stick my tail into the sand and turn myself over back onto my feet with it."

At hearing this, Bertie was relieved although that tail still looked menacing. Perhaps this monster was not as frightful as he seemed. Nonetheless, he certainly was an imposing sight as he rested before them.

"If you will excuse me," Horace added as

he began to turn away from them. "I must be getting along to my dinner now that I have made a new friend. In the future I advise you to take care to limit your swimming to the shallow water, young fellow. Now, I am off to meet my friends, the Clams, for dinner." And with that he slowly turned and began to make his way back into the water.

"Goodbye, Horace!" Bertie called after the departing creature. "And thank you again for saving my life."

Goodbye, Horace.

14

When Horace had disappeared beneath the surface of the water, Bertie turned and said, "Such a fearsome looking creature, Sebastian. No matter what he said I would still have been in fear of him if you hadn't been here." He added, "And loathsome too. How would anyone wish to marry such an ugly fellow and have children with him?"

"Oh, don't yer worry 'bout Horace findin' wives an' propagatin' the species. He's a handsome

devil, that Horace. Thur's many a female of his species what finds him most appealin'. An' as fer havin'
youngsters, why, him an' his forbearers bin around
fer millions and millions o' years; an' 'll be around
fer millions t' come, mark me words. Don't waste
yer time worryin' yer head 'bout Horace's future."

"But, Sebastian, is he really planning to
have dinner with the Clam clan? I can't imagine
that there would be enough of those tiny creatures
you told me that the clams eat to provide Horace
with a half-decent meal."

"Oh, Bertie," Sebastian chuckled. "Horace
don't plan on dinin' with the Clams; he is hopin' t'
dine *on* 'em, fer clams is his favorite food. When he
finds 'em at home he don't invite 'em out fer dinner, he digs 'em up with his many feet, opens 'em
up an' makes a good meal of 'em right on the spot."

"Oh my! Shells and all?" Bertie replied with
a grimace. "That's not my idea of a tasty dinner."

"Nor his neither. He leaves them shells behind when he's done with thur innards. He's one
o' the reasons ya sees them empty shells all over
the beach," was the gull's response, and so saying

he unfolded his left wing which he extended. He turned slowly and with a sweeping gesture indicated the broad expanse of the beach.

"Y've seen thousands of them shells strewn about all over the beach. Them's the sad remains o' many members of the Clam family 'n' other tribes what lives in shells, now gone t' a better place. Thur be many dangerous animals out here on the beach, all of 'em eager to make a meal o' large seagulls 's well 's small mice 'n' other residents here 'bouts." He added, "We got ter keep a keen eye out fer enemies the likes o' foxes 'n' coyotes 'n' skunks 'n' sech what lurks in the tall beach grass among the sand dunes, not t' mention them wicked hawks what circles overhead, jest waitin' t' swoop down 'n' carry us off if we lets our guard down fer even a moment. All around these parts y'll find dangerous critturs jest waitin' fer the chance ter make a meal o' whatever they can, fer that is how all of us stays alive."

Many had been the times that Bertie had heard stories from his parents of those dreadful enemies. Now he shivered at the thought of meeting one of them out here on the beach where there would be nowhere for him to hide if any of them saw him.

"My goodness!" exclaimed Bertie with a fearful shudder. "Now that you mention it I have noticed as we have been going along that you always seem to have one eye on the lookout."

"Righto, Bertie. We gulls be wary birds. Stayin' sharp-eyed is how we survives. Ya don't catch a seagull nappin' with his guard down very often. That's how we manages ter live fer s' long. If we goes t' sleep for even a minute while on watch we could be the makin's o' someone's dinner. Last thing ol' Sebastian wants is t' become the main course fer some four-footed fiend or flyin' foe."

"Speaking of food, I'm starting to feel a bit hungry." Bertie's tiny stomach had been grumbling softly for a while. "The thought of eating a clam or a crab is unpleasant to say the least. I think it's time for me to be getting back to my home. I have been away all morning and my mother might be wondering where I am."

"O' course. There's s' much more t' be seen

out here but we wouldn't want yer parents t' be worryin' now, would we?" Sebastian responded. "Let's change our course an' point our bows back t' them dunes."

With that they turned away from the water's edge toward the softer sand, the tall beach grass, and beyond to the path back to Bertie's home.

15

Trotting briskly along close beneath Sebastian's wing, Bertie found his mind drifting back and forth between the wonderful encounters he had enjoyed that morning, and thoughts of a delicious lunch of corn meal, oat grains and elderberry tea that awaited him at home. With any luck his parents would never suspect that he'd left the farmyard. And the tales of discovery and danger he would be able to tell his brothers and sisters and friends in the days to come! He would be careful, of course, not to speak of it to his father and mother.

She would be very distressed and might punish him for having enjoyed this daring adventure.

His imagination was working overtime. 'Such a brave young mouse was this adventurous hero.' Before long he would be the envy of the young farmyard mice. "Bertie the Bold" they would call him. How clearly he could see the future unfold in his mind's eye. There would be gala parades through the barn. An enormous dinner in celebration of Bertie the Brave would be given under the corn crib—speeches, toasts and maybe a medal! Word of his exploits would spread across the countryside and be passed down as an inspiration to future generations of young mice!

A proud smile began to spread across his face. His whiskers fairly twitched with thoughts of more adventures to come. First, he would travel to Musport to visit his cousins. From there he would find a ship and, like his father, voyage to far-off mysterious lands. There was the whole wide world out there waiting for him to explore. How good it felt to be so grown up and courageous.

'But wait!' the thought came to him with

alarm. 'What if they don't believe my tale?' In an instant his imagined fame was cut short as if a window to that new world had been slammed shut. His thoughts of a heroic life were fading quicker than a fleeting dream. After all, everyone knew that all the Fieldmouse children were forbidden to go to the beach. No one would believe his tale. He must bring back a souvenir of the morning at the beach to prove that he had, indeed, made this expedition. He could show it off and none would doubt him. Yes! That would do the trick!

They had gone just a few paces farther when he spied, just over there next to some driftwood, a shiny piece of golden seashell. It sparkled in the sun's rays, almost as if it were calling out to him, "Here I am, Bertie. I'm just the thing to make all who hear your tale believe. With me in your pocket your glorious reputation will be assured."

In a flash he had darted from beneath Sebastian's wing and was dashing across the sand toward this treasure. He skittered away so suddenly that it was a long moment before Sebastian realized that his young companion was gone. Looking

Danger plummeting earthward.

about he saw the running mouse and his goal, and at the same moment his ever-alert eye turned skyward and spotted danger plummeting earthward toward his little friend.

"Bertie, git back here at once!" he called out. "There's a hawk up there an' he's comin' straight fer yer!"

But Bertie was so intent on that gleaming shell that Sebastian's alarm went unheard. Unheedful both of the gull's warning and the rapidly descending hawk, Bertie rushed toward his prize.

16

There was no time for another word of warning. In an instant Sebastian had leaped into the air and was flying with all his might straight after Bertie. If only there was time to overtake him before that hungry hawk reached his small friend and bore him away to its nest.

But there was so little time!

Glancing upward he could see the hawk getting larger and larger as it hurtled downward toward Bertie, who was unaware of the danger above. Its wicked hooked claws gaped wide. It would swoop down, snatch Bertie without even touching the sand and soar away before Sebastian could get there to protect him.

Now Sebastian was just feet away from Bertie; but the hawk, too, had almost reached the unwitting mouse.

It was going be close!

So close!

He saw now that there would be no time to shield Bertie from the streaking hawk.

Now the hawk was reaching out with its talons. Its great wings, spread wide, acted as air brakes to slow its tremendous downward speed.

It was the sound of wind rushing past the streaking hawk's feathers that caused Bertie to turn his head and look upward. There were those dreadful talons spread wide, only a few feet away from his now-cringing face.

The terrible thought flooded into his mind. 'Oh, dear. This surely must be the end for me!'

Cowering low he pressed himself into the sand.

He pressed himself into the sand.

So focused was he on those onrushing claws that he was unaware of Sebastian, also only a few feet away.

Too late for Sebastian to hurl himself between Bertie and that demon hawk! He did the only thing he could. In full flight he barreled straight into the lunging hawk. The two birds came together with a tremendous WHUNK!!!

What a collision! Feathers flew in all directions as both Sebastian and the hawk tumbled head over feet through the air before both fell to the sand just a short distance from the trembling mouse.

17

Brown hawk plumage and white gull feathers floated down all around him. Over there lay his battered friend motionless in the sand, his wings and legs every which way. Farther off lay the unmoving hawk.

"Oh dear! What have I done?!" moaned Bertie. "What a foolish mouse I am! My friend is dead because of me," and he scurried over to the gull who lay on the sand with his feathers all awry.

He gently touched the gull's cheek.

He continued in a piteous voice, "Oh, Sebastian, I am so sorry. Please do not be dead," and reaching out he gently touched the gull's cheek with a hesitant paw. "If you are dead I shall never be able to forgive myself." A tear trickled from each eye. How terrible to be responsible for Sebastian's death, and all because he had wanted that bright shell so that he could puff himself up to his friends.

Overcome with sadness and remorse, he

sat down in the sand beside the motionless gull and began to weep in a flood of anguished sorrow. "My parents were right. Coming to the beach was surely the worst idea I have ever had."

What would he do now? His friend, dreadfully injured and perhaps dead, and he, Bertie, so far from home in a land full of dangerous beasts eager to make a meal of him. He felt both lost and fearful and looked all around and into the sky to see if more danger was in the offing.

"Oh woe, woe, woe is me. Whatever shall I do now?" he groaned, his tear-drenched face turned upward to the blue sky overhead.

And then, as he was sadly caressing Sebastian's brow, he saw the gull's eyelid flutter and in another moment later open wide.

"Ah, Bertie, me foolish little friend, how good t' see yer safe 'n' sound," Sebastian said in a quavery voice.

"Oh, Sebastian, you are alive," Bertie exclaimed joyfully. "Thank goodness you are alive! Are you all right?"

"Well, let's have a look at meself," replied the gull and, taking a deep breath, he got painfully to his feet and stretched his legs and wings.

"ARRRGGGHHH!" he let out a long groan. "Shiver me timbers Bertie, I'm wracked from me foretop t' me keel!" then let out another groan before adding, "That were some collision, an' a close call fer yerself, 's well, lad. But it appears we're both alive an' kickin,' thank our stars!"

"Oh, Sebastian," Bertie declared sorrowfully, "What a fool I've been. Can you ever forgive me for such an awful mistake? What I did could have killed us both." He asked hesitatingly, "Are you alright?"

" 'All's well s' long 's the battle's done an' we're still afloat,' as the sayin' goes, shipmate, but that last shot loosened me planks some." He groaned once again, though not quite so painfully, before adding, as he got to his feet, "Let me survey me hull an' sails ter find out if everythin's still in workin' condition."

He grimaced as, one at a time, he painfully

stretched each wing and then each leg, before he re-marked, "Give me a minute while I check me movin' parts 'n' runnin' riggin' t' see if all's in order."

With that he leaped ungracefully into the air and rose in an awkward circle on rickety wings. But the next moment he was flying easily, and in another, he had returned in a swift swoop and landed beside Bertie.

"Everythin' aboard seems t' be ship shape. It'll take more 'n fetchin' up hard agin' Henry Hawk t' do me in. We gulls is made o' stern stuff."

I don't know if we can say the same for that awful bird," replied Bertie, pointing to the hawk, who still lay motionless nearby on the sand.

"I'm thinkin' we'd best not be tarryin' here t' find out the state o' his health. We needs ter get yer back t' yer family afore somethin' else happens. I've a notion we'd best be deliverin' yer t' yer home by air mail that'll be the safest way."

"By air!?" exclaimed the mouse. "What do you mean?"

"Why, Bertie, just yer hop on ter me back

and I'll fly yer home quicker 'n yer can say 'Jack Robinson.' "

"But that can't be safe! What if I should fall?"

"Jest hold tight ter me feathers and everything'll be okay."

"Well… if you say so. But, Sebastian, might we bring that along within us?" He pointed to the shiny gold shell that lay in the sand at his feet.

"Of course y' may," was the gull's reply.

Bertie hurried to pick up his glittering prize. Clutching it in his paws he returned to the gull with a gleeful bound. Another hop and he was astride Sebastian with the shell tucked securely between his chest and Sebastian's back. With both front paws and all his toes he tightly grasped the gull's feathers.

"All set fer take off, Bertie?"

" I g-g-g-g-guess so."

With that Sebastian gave a mighty leap and they were airborne.

He clung to the gull's back with all his strength.

18

Bertie eyes were shut tightly as he clung to the gull's back with all his strength. The wind whistled in his ears and rushed against his eyes as they soared aloft. It pushed into his nose. His whiskers fluttered wildly against his cheeks so that he didn't dare to open his eyes.

'Oh my! This is a dreadful mistake,' he

thought. 'This flight may be the greatest adventure of my life and I don't even dare to look! I am a foolish little mouse.' With that he opened his eyes to take in the view. No beach or beach grass or hills or trees were to be seen. All he could see was the blue and empty sky. Turning his head to his right he glanced down. The beach below seemed to be falling away beneath them. Everything was growing smaller. He could not make out the hawk and the spot where his life had so nearly ended.

There was so much down there to see. To his right and far over there the blue sea met the sand. To his left the sand met with the tall beach grass. And there! He thought he could make out the opening to the path that led back to the farm and his home. They were almost directly above it. It looked so tiny.

He could feel the strong regular movement of Sebastian's beating wing muscles under him. How easy this flying seemed for his friend. How marvelous it must be to be able to come up here whenever you wished, to be free from having to walk and run on the ground.

Bertie could make out the familiar
apple orchard.

19

And now, although his wings had stopped moving, Sebastian seemed to be soaring ever higher into the sky. They glided smoothly along without a hint of effort on the part of the gull. Far below Bertie could make out the familiar apple orchard and over there were the old barn and farmhouse.

"Are y' doin' okay, Bertie?" he heard the gull call to him over the noise of the wind in his ears. "Not scared, are ya?"

"I'm fine, Sebastian," he called back into the rushing wind. "This flying is wonderful. It's even better than swimming. How I wish I could do this by myself."

"Better not try it until y've grown a pair o' wings," Sebastian chuckled. "And if yer ever acquires 'em y'd be needin' to do a bit o' practicin' afore y' try this. Hold on tight now, we're goin' down."

And with that he dipped his left wing and they were suddenly, frightfully, diving toward the ground. The wind shrieked past Bertie's ears. He was holding on for dear life again. For a moment he shut his eyes in terror. But only for a moment. When he opened them he could see that the apple orchard was rushng toward them at an alarming speed.

'Oh no!' Bertie thought. 'After the narrow escapes I have had this morning we are going to crash into an apple tree! Oh dear! Dear! Dear!'

20

Then, as it seemed they would certainly fly headlong into the tree branches, Sebastian did something with his wings and instantly they were no longer speeding earthward. The next thing Bertie knew they were gliding calmly just above the apple trees toward the barn, the cornfield, and, yes, the old fence posts. In another moment Sebastian had floated easily to earth and landed gently on the brown earth at the edge of the field.

"Well, here y' are, Bertie, me good friend, home again all ther same day, safe an' sound."

"Oh, Sebastian, I was certain I was a goner back there," declared Bertie, now recovered from his most recent fright.

"We didn't come close to them trees. It might o' seemed that way to yer fer y're not used to goin' s' fast an' don't know how easy it is fer me to change directions. Now, jest hop yerself down an' run along to yer home afore yer mother sees us here an' suspects what y've been up ter. It's bin a most enjoyable mornin' fer me."

"Dear Sebastian, my friend," said Bertie. "Thank you ever so much for my awesome adventure. I'll remember this day, and you, forever. I've learned so much about that wonderful beach where you and your friends live. I'm a wiser mouse now; from now on I will listen to the advice of those who are more experienced than I."

"Good fer you, me little friend. An' remember t' keep yer wits about yer an' a sharp lookout at all times. 'Tis a dangerous world we lives in."

Bertie jumped from the gull's back to the ground, turned to look up at the old gull and touch his breast one last time. After a final glance down-

"Goodbye and thank you, Sebastian."

ward at his friend, Sebastian spread his wings wide, gave a strong push with his legs and vaulted into the air.

Bertie waved and called out "Goodbye, and thank you, Sebastian."

Then, clutching his seashell tightly he turned and hurried to his family's cozy home.

What a morning!

THE END

About the Author

When John Hutchinson was a small child his mother often entertained him with a story of a young mouse's first visit to the seashore. John carried her short tale in his memory for 70 years, eventually deciding to put it down in book form.

Bertie's Adventure At the Beach is an elaboration of his recollection of her story. The illustrations are from the hand of his talented daughter Scout and him.

John Hutchinson is a well-known artist who lives in Massachusetts on Cape Cod, where he enjoys his own beach adventures with his dog, Jazzy. He is currently working on a second book which tells of Bertie's search for pirate treasure on Skull Island.